ACOUSTIC TROUBADOURS

Contents

ISBN 1-57560-588-0

Copyright © 2003 Cherry Lane Music Company
International Copyright Secured All Rights Reserved

The music, text, design and graphics in this publication are protected by copyright law.
Any duplication or transmission, by any means, electronic, mechanical, photocopying,
recording or otherwise, is an infringement of copyright.

Visit our website at www.cherrylane.com

CALIFORNIA

Words and Music by
Rufus Wainwright

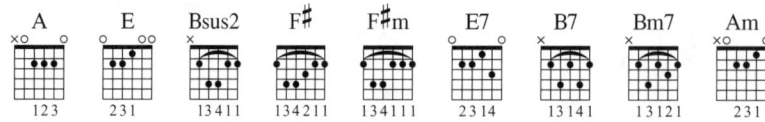

Copyright © 2001 DreamWorks Songs (ASCAP) and Rock And Roll Credit Card Music (ASCAP)
Worldwide Rights for DreamWorks Songs and Rock And Roll Credit Card Music Administered by Cherry Lane Music Publishing Company, Inc.
International Copyright Secured   All Rights Reserved

1st time, Gtr. 1: w/ Rhy. Fig. 1 (last 4 meas.)
1st time, Gtr. 2 tacet
2nd time, Gtrs. 1 & 2: w/ Rhy. Fig. 1 (1st 3 meas.)
F♯m
Bsus2
A
E
whiffs of fre - on,
and big nights back east with Rho - da.
and my new grand - ma, Bea Ar - thur.
A
E
1.
Bsus2
Gtr. 2
Cal - i - for - nia, please.
Come on o - ver.
2.
Bridge
Bkgd. Voc.: w/ Voc. Fig. 1
E7
Gtrs. 1 & 2
B7
Rhy. Fig. 2
Ain't it a shame that at the top pea -
B7
- nut but - ter and jam they served you. Ain't it a shame
(...jam they served you.)
Bm7
that at the top still those soft - skin boys.
(...boys
Voc. Fig. 1
Oo, oo, oo.

A
Am
E
End Rhy. Fig. 2
Gtr. 1
(Gtr. 2 cont. in notation)
can bruise you, yeah. I fell for a
can bruise you.)
Fill 1
End Fill 1
Gtr. 2
(cont. in slashes)
F♯m
B7
Gtrs. 1 & 2
streak - er, oh no.
Gtr. 3 (elec.)
mf
let ring
let ring
sim.
1/2
Guitar Solo
Gtrs. 1 & 2: w/ Rhy. Fig. 1
A
E
w/ delay
Bsus2

Verse

3. I don't know this sea of ne-on, thou-sand surf-ers, whiffs of fre-on.

Bridge

Ain't it a shame that all the world can't en-joy your mad tra-di-tions. (...mad tra-di-tions.) Ain't it a shame that all the world don't got keys to their own ig-ni-tions. Life (...own ig-ni-tions.)

is the long - est death in Cal-i-for - nia.

Outro

(Oo, oo.)

A E Bsus2
You're such a won - der that I think I'll stay in bed.
End Riff A
Gtr. 3: w/ Riff A (2 1/2 times)
A E A E A E
(Oo, oo.)
So much to plun - der that I
Bsus2 A E A E
think I'll sleep in - stead.
(Oo, oo.)
A E Bsus2 A E
You're such a won - der that I think I'll stay in bed.
(Oo,
Slower, freely
A E A E B7
Gtr. 2
oo.)
So much to plun - der that I think I'll
Gtr. 1
Am E
Gtr. 1
(cont. in notation)
molto rit.
sleep in - stead.
Gtr. 2
let ring
(cont. in slashes)
molto rit.

THE CHRISTIANS AND THE PAGANS

Written by
Dar Williams

Gtr. 1: Capo I

Intro

Moderate Folk Rock ♩ = 105

* Symbols in parentheses represent chord names respective to capoed guitar.
Symbols above reflect actual sounding chords. Capoed fret is "0" in TAB.
† Chord symbols reflect overall tonality.

𝄋 Verse

1. Am-ber called her un-cle, said, "We're up _ here for _ the hol-i-day,_ Jane.
food was great, the tree plugged in, the meal _ had gone _ with-out _ a hitch, 'til
3. *See Additional Lyrics*

Rhy. Fig. 1

simile on repeat

© 1995 BURNING FIELD MUSIC (ASCAP) /Administered by BUG MUSIC
All Rights Reserved   Used by Permission

and I,____ we're hav - ing Sol - stice, now ____ we need __ a place __
Tim - my turned_ to Am - ber and said, "Is it true ___ that you're _

___ to stay."
___ a witch?"
And her Christ ___ lov - ing un - cle watched his
His mom jumped up and said,"The pies _____ are

End Rhy. Fig. 1

wife hang Mar - y on __ a tree. __ He watched his son hang can - dy canes_ all
burn - ing." And she hit __ the kitch - en. And it was Jane who spoke, she said, "It's

made with red ___ dye num - ber three. He
true your cous - in's not _____ a Chris - tian." _____ "But

8

Gtr. 1: w/ Rhy. Fig. 1, simile

Ab (G)   Db (C)   Bbm (Am)   Eb (D)

told his niece, "It's Christ - mas Eve, __ I know __ our life __ is not __ your style." She said,
we love trees, we love __ the snow, the friends __ we have, the world we share. And

Ab (G)   Db (C)   Bbm (Am)   Eb (D)

"Christ-mas is like Sol - stice, and we miss __ you and it's been __ a - while." __
you find mag-ic from _ your God, and we ___ find _ mag - ic ev - 'ry - where."

So the Christ-

1.

Chorus

Ab (G)   Db (C)   Fm (Em)   Eb (D)

- tians and __ the Pa - gans sat __ to _ geth - er at __ the ta - ble.

Gtr. 1   **Rhy. Fig. 2**

Ab (G)   Db (C)   Fm (Em)   Eb (D)

Find-ing faith _ and com - mon ground _ the best ___ that they _ were a - ble. And

Fm (Em)   Db (C)   Bbm (Am)   Eb (D)

just be - fore __ the meal __ was served, __ hands were held __ and prayers ___ were said.

mf

9

Fm (Em)   Db (C)   Bbm (Am)   Eb (D)

Send - ing hope _ for peace _ on Earth _ to all ____ their gods _ and god -

Ab (G)

dess - es.   2. The

End Rhy. Fig. 2

2.

Chorus

Gtr. 1: w/ Rhy. Fig. 2, 1st time
Gtr. 1: w/ Rhy. Fig. 2, 1st 9 meas., 2nd time

Ab (G)   Db (C)   Fm (Em)   Eb (D)

- tians and _ the Pa - gans sat _ to - geth - er at __ the ta - ble.

(The Chris - tians,   the Pa - gans,   to - geth - er,   oh, woah. ___

Ab (G)   Db (C)   Fm (Em)   Eb (D)

Find-ing faith _ and com - mon ground _ the best ___ that they _ were a - ble.

Hal - le - lu - jah,   hal - le,   oh, woah. _____

Fm (Em)　Db (C)　Bbm (Am)　Eb (D)

Where does mag - ic come _ from? I think ma - gic's in _ the learn-ing. 'Cause now when _
Light - ing trees in dark - ness, learn - ing new ways from _ the old. ___ And

Woah, ___ woah, woah, ___

Fm (Em)　Db (C)　Bbm (Am)　Eb (D)

Chris - tians sit _ with Pa - gans on - ly pump - kin pies _ are burn -
mak - ing sense of his - to - ry, and draw - ing warmth _ out of ___

woah.

To Coda ⊕

D.S. al Coda
(take 2nd ending)

Ab (G)

ing. ___
the cold. _
_)

3. When

⊕ Coda
Outro

Ab (G)　Db (C)　Eb9sus4/C (D9sus4/B)　Bbm (Am)　Eb (D)　Ab (G)

Gtr. 1

Additional Lyrics

3. When Amber tried to do the dishes, her aunt said, "Really, no, don't bother."
Amber's uncle saw how Amber looked like Tim and like her father.
He thought about his brother, how they hadn't spoken in a year,
He thought he'd call him up and say, "It's Christmas and your daughter's here."
He thought of fathers, sons and brothers, saw his own son tug his sleeve, saying,
"Can I be a Pagan?" Dad said, "We'll discuss it when they leave."

11

COUNTRY ROAD

Words and Music by
James Taylor

© 1970 (Renewed 1998) EMI BLACKWOOD MUSIC INC. and COUNTRY ROAD MUSIC INC.
All Rights Controlled and Administered by EMI BLACKWOOD MUSIC INC.
All Rights Reserved   International Copyright Secured   Used by Permission

one and _ the same.   Ma-ma don't un - der-stand it.   She wants to know where_ I've been.   I'd
have your own choice.   But I can see   a heav-en-ly band full of an - gels com-in' to set _ me free.   I

have to be some_ kind of nat-'ral   born fool to want to pass   that   way a - gain,_ but you know I could feel_
don't know noth-ing _ 'bout the why or   when but I can   tell you that it's bound to be _   be- cause I could feel_

To Coda ⊕

_ it,   }
_ it child, yeah! }   on a coun-try road. _

|1.

|2.

13

Interlude

I guess my feet __ know where they _ want me to go, _____ walk-ing on a coun-try road.

D.S. al Coda

Coda   Outro

Walk on   down, _ walk on ___ down, _ walk on   down, _

14

walk on __ down, __ walk-ing on a coun-try road. __

La la la la __ la la la la la la __ la la __ la la la la la la la la __

__ la la la la, __ coun-try road. __ Woah! __ Yeah! __

Walk-ing on a coun-try road. __

Coun-try road.

Whew! Coun-try road.

Fade

DOG & BUTTERFLY

Words and Music by
Ann Wilson, Nancy Wilson
and Sue Ennis

Intro
Moderately slow ♩ = 62

*Gtr. 1

Asus2

mf
let ring throughout

*Two 12-str. acous. gtrs. arr. for one.

Verse

Aadd9

1. There I was __ with the old __ man, stranded a-gain, so off I ran. __ A
2., 3. *See additional lyrics*

E

Asus2

young world crash-ing a-round me, __ no pos-si-bil-i-ties of get-ting what I need. __ He

E

C#7

F#m

looked at me, __ smiled, __ said, "No, __ no, __ no, no, __ no, __

B

Bsus4   B   Bsus2   A/B

Copyright © 1978 Strange Euphoria Music and Know Music (ASCAP)
International Copyright Secured   All Rights Reserved

Chorus
D E Asus2
child." See the dog and but-ter-fly, up in the
Rhy. Fig. 1
To Coda
Amaj9(no3rd) G5 Dsus2
air he like to fly. Dog and but-ter-fly. Be-
End Rhy. Fig. 1
Asus2 Amaj9 F♯m C♯m
low, she had to try. She rolled back down to the warm, soft ground laugh-
Rhy. Fill 1
End Rhy. Fill 1
1.
F♯m B Bsus4 Dsus2
-ing, she don't know why, she don't know why. Dog and but-ter-fly.
Rhy. Fill 2
End Rhy. Fill 2

Amaj9(no3rd)
Aadd9
2. Well, I
2.
Gtr. 1: w/ Rhy. Fill 2
F♯m
B
Bsus4
Dsus2
-ing to the sky,
up to the sky.
Dog and but-ter-fly.
Bridge
Amaj9(no3rd)
N.C.
C♯m
F♯m
Dsus2
Asus2
We're get-ting old-er,
the world's get-ting cold-er,
for the
Gtr. 1
D
Gmaj7
Asus2
N.C.
life of me
I don't know the rea-son why.
C♯m
F♯m
Dsus2
Asus2
May-be it's liv-in'
mak-ing us give in.

Hearts roll-ing in, ta - ken back on the tide. We're

bal-anced to-geth - er, o - cean up - on the sky.

D.S. al Coda

3. An -

⊕ **Coda**

Gtr. 1: w/ Rhy. Fill 1

low, she had to try. And she rolled back down to the warm, soft ground with a lit-tle
(She had to try. Rolled back down to the ground.)

20

F♯m
B
tear in her eye. Yeah. She had to try,
...in her eye.)
Gtr. 1
Rhy. Fill 3
Bsus4
Dsus2
she had to try dog and but - ter - fly.
(Dog and but - ter - fly.
End Rhy. Fill 3
Gtr. 1: w/ Rhy. Fig. 1
Asus2
Amaj9(no3rd)
Yeah. Up in the air he like to fly. The
Up in the air he like to fly.
G5
Dsus2
Gtr. 1: w/ Rhy. Fill 1
Asus2
Amaj9
dog and but - ter - fly. Be - low, she had to try. And she rolled
Dog and but - ter - fly. Be - low, she had to try.

Gtr. 1: w/ Rhy. Fill 3

F#m   C#m   F#m   B

____ back down _ to the warm,_ soft ground _   laugh-ing,   she don't know   why,_____   but she had ___ to try,_
_____ Rolled _ back down _ to the ground.)_

Bsus4   Dsus2

____ yeah,   she had _____ to   try ____   dog and   but - ter - fly. _____
     (Dog and   but - ter - fly.) _____

Outro

Repeat and fade

Asus2

_____ Ooh. ____   Ooh, ooh, ooh, ooh, ooh,   ooh._

Gtr. 1

Additional Lyrics

2. Well, I stumbled upon your secret place.
   Safe in the trees, you had tears on your face.
   Wrestling with your desires.
   The frozen stranger stealing your fires.
   The message hit my mind.
   Only words that I could find. *(To Chorus)*

3. Another night in this strange town.
   Moonlight holdin' me light as down.
   Voice of confusion inside of me
   Just beggin' to go back where I'm free.
   Feels like I'm through,
   Then the old man's words are true. *(To Chorus)*

FLAKE

Words and Music by
Jack Johnson

Gtrs. 3 & 4: Open E tuning, capo I:
(low to high) E-B-E-G♯-B-E

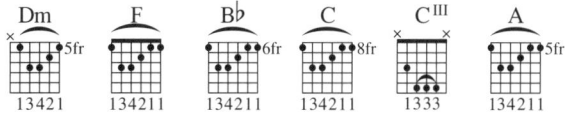

Intro

Moderately slow ♩ = 100

1. I know she said it's al-right, but you can make it up next time. I know she knows it's not right, there ain't no use in ly-ing. May-be she thinks I know something, may-be, may-be she thinks it's fine. May-be she knows some-thing I don't. I'm so, I'm so ti-red, I'm so tired of try-ing.

Chorus

It seems to me that "may - be," *Gtr. 2 (acous.) played mp.

Copyright © 2000 by Bubble Toes Publishing (ASCAP)
All Rights Reserved   Used by Permission

Dm · · · · · · · · A · · · · · · · ·

it pret-ty much al-ways means_____ "no." So don't_____

B♭ · · · · · · · · C · · · · · · · ·

_____ tell_____ me_____ you might just let_____ it go._____

F · · · · · · · · C · · · · · · · ·

End Rhy. Fig. 2

_____

Gtrs. 1 & 2: w/ Rhy. Fig. 2
F   C   Dm   A

And of-ten-times we're la - zy,____ it seems to stand in my____ way.____ 'Cause

B♭   C   F   C

no one, no,_____ not no_____ one likes to be let down.____

Verse
Gtr. 2 tacet
Dm   F   B♭   F

Gtrs.
1 & 2   Gtr. 1

2. I know she loves the sun - rise, no long-er sees it with her sleep-ing eyes__ and...

Dm   F   B♭   F

I know that when she said she's gon-na try,__ well, it might not work be-cause of oth-er ties__ and...

Gtr. 1: w/ Rhy. Fig. 1 (1 3/4 times)
Dm   F   B♭

3

I know she u-su-al-ly has some oth-er ties__ and, ah, I would-n't want to break 'em, nah,

F   Dm   F

I would-n't want to break 'em. May-be she'll help me to un-tie____ this, but

24

Chorus
Gtr. 1: w/ Rhy. Fill 1
Gtrs. 1 & 2: w/ Rhy. Fig. 2 (3 times)
B♭ C F
un - til then, well, I'm gon - na have to lie, too. It seems to me that "may -
C Dm A
- be," it pret - ty much al - ways means "no." So don't
B♭ C F
tell me you might just let it go.
C *(B) F (E) C (B)
And of - ten times we're la - zy,
Gtr. 3 (dobro)
Riff A
mp w/ slide & fingers
*Symbols in parentheses represent chord names respective to capoed guitar. Symbols above reflect actual sounding chord. Capoed fret is "0" in tab.
Dm (C♯m) A (G♯) B♭ (A)
it seems to stand in my way. 'Cause no one, no, not no
C (B) F (E) C (B)
one likes to be let down.
End Riff A

It seems to me that "may - be," __ it pret-ty much al - ways means __ "no." So don't __

__ tell __ me __ you might just let __ it go. __

(The)

26

Outro
F
(E)
B♭
(A)
harder that you try, baby, the further you'll fall, even with all
Gtr. 3
mp
Rhy. Fig. 4A
Gtr. 4
Rhy. Fig. 4
Gtr. 1
F
(E)
C
(B)
the money in the whole wide world.

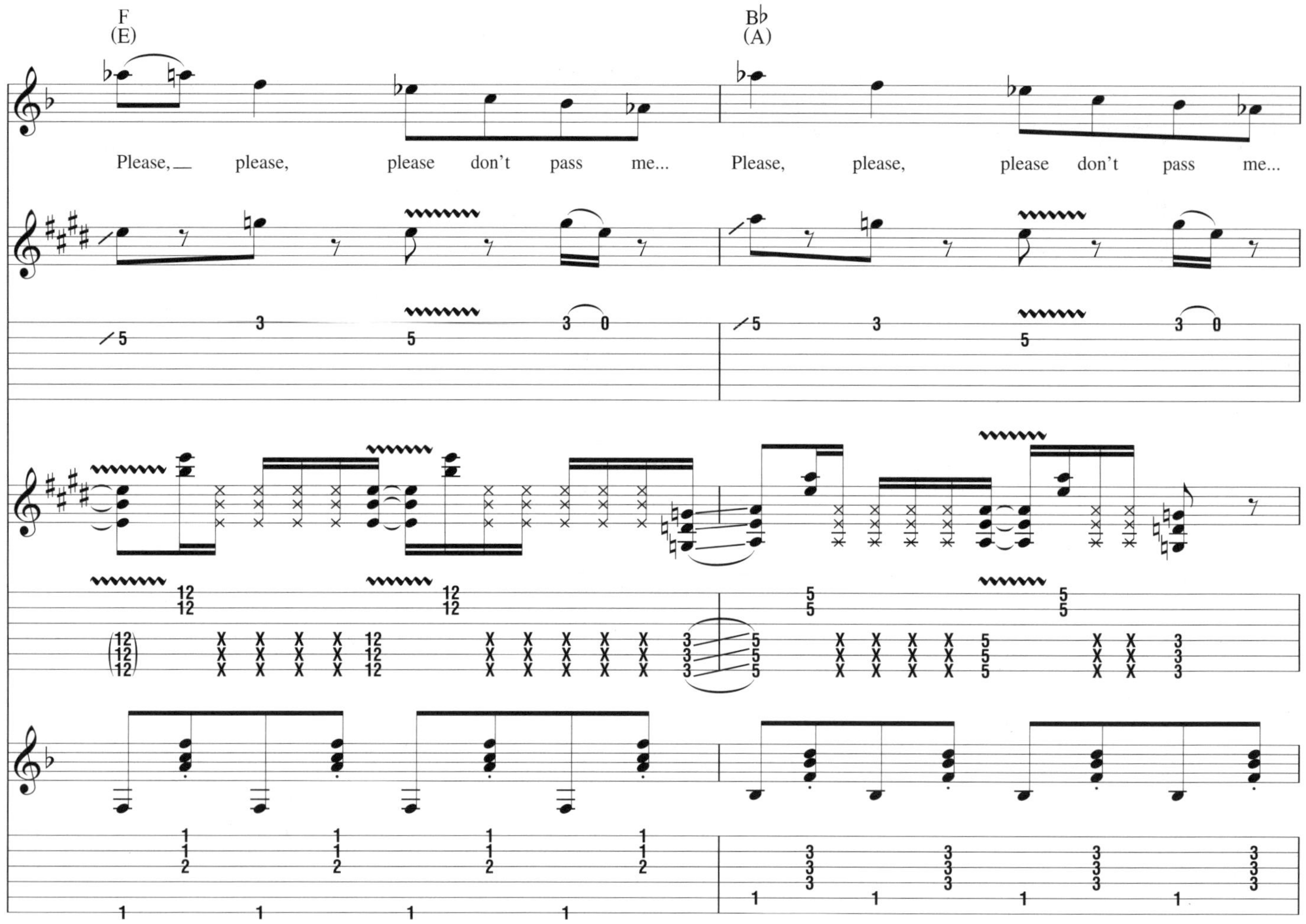
F
(E)
B♭
(A)
Please, please, please don't pass me... Please, please, please don't pass me...

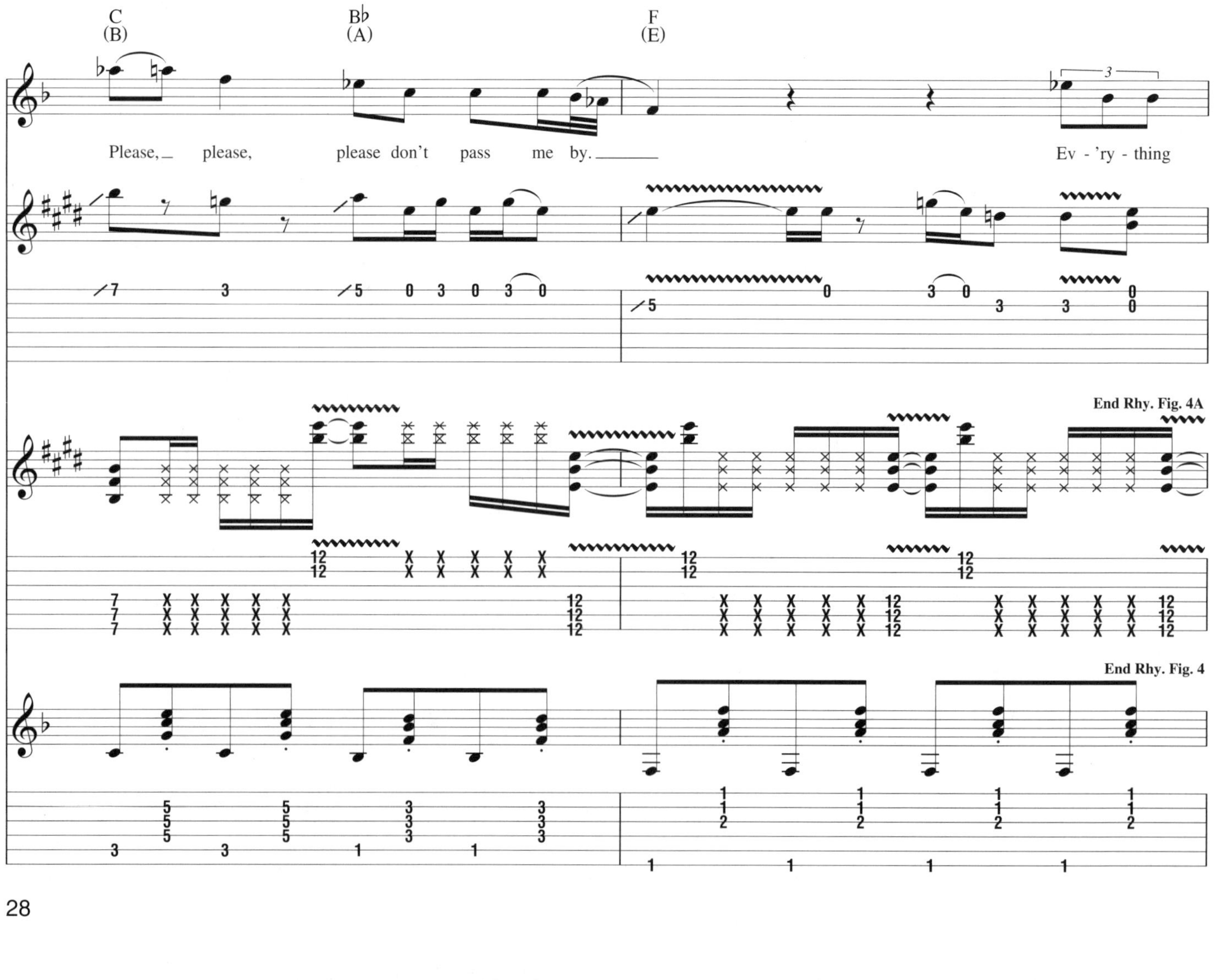
C
(B)
B♭
(A)
F
(E)
Please, please, please don't pass me by. Ev - 'ry - thing
End Rhy. Fig. 4A
End Rhy. Fig. 4

Gtrs. 1 & 4: w/ Rhy. Figs. 4 & 4A (2 times)
B♭ (A)
you know a - bout me now, ba - by, you gon - na have to change, you gon - na call
Gtr. 3
Gtr. 3 tacet
F (E)
C (B)
it by a brand - new name, oo, oo, oo.
F (E)
B♭ (A)
Please, please, please don't drag me... Please, please, please don't drag me...
Gtr. 3
C (B)
B♭ (A)
F (E)
Please, please, please don't drag me down. Just like a tree
Gtr. 3 tacet
B♭ (A)
down by the wa - ter, ba - by, I shall not move, e - ven af - ter all

the sil-ly things you do, oo, oo, oo.

Please, please, please don't drag me... Please, please, please don't drag me...

Please, please, please don't drag me down.

FROM A DISTANCE

Gtr. 2 chords (A) (D) (E) (F#m) (Esus4) (Aadd4)

234 232 231 3111 234 34

Gtr. 3 chords ((C))

32 1

Gtr. 2: Capo V
Gtr. 3: Capo II

Words and Music by
Julie Gold

Intro

Moderately ♩ = 90

Gtr. 4: w/ Fill 1

Dadd2   A/C#   Bm7add4   A   G6/9
*(Aadd2) (E/G#) (F#m7add4) (E)   (D6/9)
*((Cadd2)) ((G/B)) ((Am7add4)) ((G)) ((F6/9))

Dadd2   A/C#   Bm7add4   A   G6/9
(Aadd2) (E/G#) (F#m7add4) (E)   (D6/9)
((Cadd2)) ((G/B)) ((Am7add4)) ((G)) ((F6/9))

1. From a

Gtr. 1 (elec.)   Riff A   End Riff A

mf
w/ clean tone

Gtr. 2 (12-str. acous.)   Riff B   End Riff B

mf
(cont. in slashes)

Gtr. 3 (acous.)

mf

*Symbols in parentheses represent chord names respective to capoed Gtr. 2.
Symbols in double parentheses represent chord names respective to capoed Gtr. 3.
Symbols above reflect actual sounding chords. Capoed fret is "0" in tab.

Fill 1
*Gtr. 4 (acous.)

8va
mf A.H.
T
17

*Mandolin arr. for gtr.

Copyright © 1986, 1987 Julie Gold Music (BMI) and Wing & Wheel Music (BMI)
Julie Gold Music Administered Worldwide by Cherry River Music Co.
Wing & Wheel Music Administered Worldwide by Irving Music, Inc.
International Copyright Secured All Rights Reserved

Verse
A D E A D E
Gtr. 2
dis - tance, the world looks blue and green and the snow - capped moun - tains
Gtr. 1
Gtr. 3
let ring
let ring
sim.
Gtr. 4: w/ Fill 2
A E A D
open
white. From a dis - tance, the o - cean meets

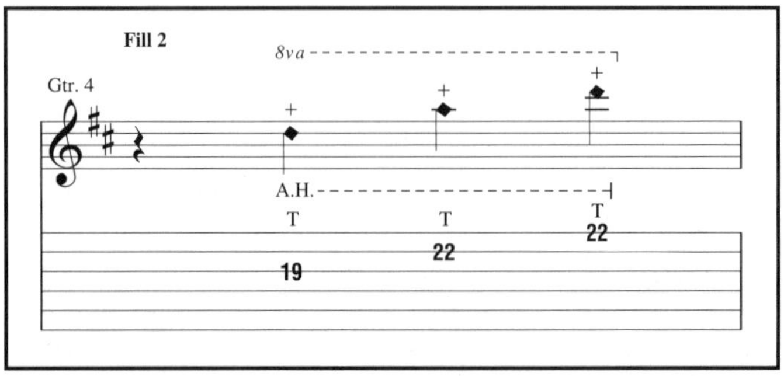
Fill 2
Gtr. 4
8va
A.H.
T
T
T

the stream,___ and the ea - gle ___ takes ___ to flight.___

Chorus

From___ a dis - tance, there ___ is har - mo - ny, ___ and it

33

Lyrics:
ech-oes through the land. It's the voice of hope; it's the voice of peace; it's the voice of ev-'ry man. 2. From a

Chorus

Gtr. 2: w/ Rhy. Fig. 1
Gtr. 3: w/ Rhy. Fig. 1A

Asus4 (Esus4) ((Gsus4))
A (E) ((G))
G (D) ((F))
D (A) ((C))
G (D) ((F))
D (A) ((C))
play - in' songs of hope, play - in' songs of peace. They're the
G (D) ((F))
A (E) ((G))
Gtr. 3: w/ Rhy. Fill 1
A
Gtr. 3: w/ Rhy. Fig. 1A (1st 2 meas.)
D
E
Gtr. 2
songs of ev - 'ry man. God is watch - ing us. God is
Rhy. Fill 1
Gtr. 3

Gtr. 3: w/ Rhy. Fig. 1A (last meas.)

F#m ... D ... E

(cont. in notation)

watch - ing us._____ God is watch - ing us from a

Gtr. 1: w/ Riff A

Dadd2	A/C#	Bm7add4	A	G§
(Aadd2)	(E/G#)	(F#m7add4)	(E)	(D§)
((Cadd2))	((G/B))	((Am7add4))	((G))	((F§))

dis - tance.

Gtr. 4

Gtr. 2

Gtr. 3

3. From   a

Riff C
End Riff C

Verse
Gtr. 3: w/ Rhy. Fig. 2
Gtr. 4 tacet

dis - tance,   you ___ look ___ like ___   my   friend, ___   e - ven   though ___ we ___ are ___   at   war. ___

Gtr. 2

Gtr. 1

Gtrs. 2 & 3: w/ Rhy. Fill 2
Gtr. 2: w/ Rhy. Fig. 1 (last 3 meas.)
Gtr. 3: w/ Rhy. Fig. 1A (last 3 meas.)
Bm (F♯m) ((Am))
G (D) ((F))
D (A) ((C))
It's the hope of hopes; it's the
8va
loco
G (D) ((F))
D (A) ((C))
G (D) ((F))
A (E) ((G))
love of loves; it's the song of ev - 'ry man.

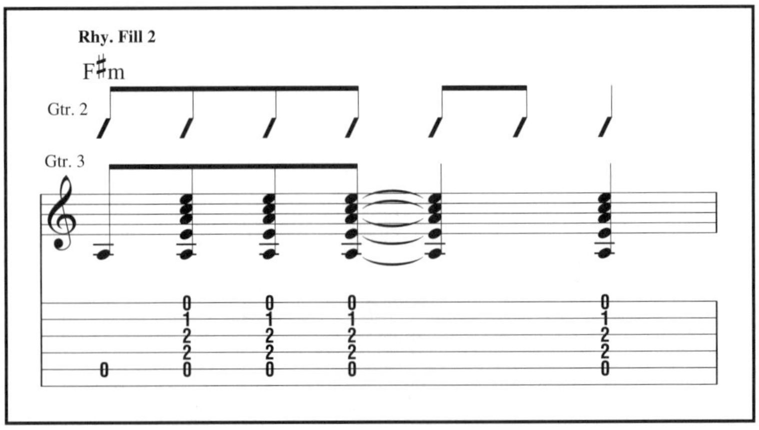

Rhy. Fill 2
F♯m
Gtr. 2
Gtr. 3

Outro
Gtr. 1: w/ Riff A (1st 2 meas.) (4 times)
Gtr. 3: w/ Riff C (4 times)
Dadd2 (Aadd2) ((Cadd2))
A/C♯ (E/G♯) ((G/B))
Bm7add4 (F♯m7add4) ((Am7add4))
A (E) ((G))
G6/9 (D6/9) ((F6/9))
Gtr. 4
Gtr. 2
C
Gtr. 3
Gtr. 4
Gtr. 1
divisi

GREENSLEEVES

Arranged by
James Taylor

Gtr. 1: Capo III

A Freely (♩ = ca. 184)

* Symbols in parentheses represent chord names respective to capoed guitar. Symbols above reflect
  actual sounding chords. Capoed fret is "0" in TAB. Chord symbols reflect implied harmony.

© 1969, 1971 (Renewed 1997, 1999) EMI BLACKWOOD MUSIC INC. and COUNTRY ROAD MUSIC
All Rights Controlled and Administered by EMI BLACKWOOD MUSIC INC.
All Rights Reserved   International Copyright Secured   Used by Permission

HELPLESSLY HOPING

Words and Music by
Stephen Stills

Help - less - ly hop - ing her har - le - quin hov - ers near -

by, a - wait - ing a word..

* Strum w/index finger.

Copyright © 1969 Gold Hill Music Inc.
Copyright Renewed
All Rights Administered by Sony/ATV Music Publishing, 8 Music Square West, Nashville, TN 37203
International Copyright Secured All Rights Reserved

Gasp - ing at glimp - ses_ of gen - tle_ true spir - it, he

runs, wish - ing he_ could fly._____

On - ly to trip_ at the sound_ of_ good - bye._

(end Rhy. Fig. 1)

2nd Verse
w/Rhy. Fig. 1

Am7 ... C

Word - less - ly watch - ing__ he__ waits by the win -

G   C/G   G

dow_____ and won - ders at the emp - ty place__ in - side.__

D   Am7

Heart - less - ly help - ing__ him -

C   G   C/G   G   C/G

self to her bad__ dreams he wor - ies, did he__ hear a good -

D   Am7   C

bye_____ or ev - en_____ hel - lo?__

G   G7sus4   Chorus
G

Rhy. Fig. 1A- - - - - - - - - - - - - - - - - - - -
They are one__   per-

Gsus4   G5   Gsus4

son. They are two__   a - lone._____ They are three__

G5　　Gsus4　　G5　　G7

to-geth - er. They are for＿＿＿＿＿＿＿＿＿ each

Csus2　　　　　　G

oth - er.

3rd Verse
w/Rhy. Fig. 1
Am7　　　　　　C

Stand by the stair - way＿ you'll＿ see some - thing cer - tain＿ to tell＿

G　C/G　G　　　D

＿ you, con-fu - sion has＿ it's costs.＿

Am7　　　　　C

Love is-n't ly - ing＿ it's loose＿ in a la - dy who ling -

G　　C/G　　G　　C/G　　D

ers say - ing she＿ is lost＿＿＿＿＿ and

w/Rhy. Fig. 1A
Am7　　C　　　　G

chok - ing＿＿＿＿ on hel - lo.{＿＿＿＿＿＿＿＿＿＿＿＿＿＿
They are one＿

49

I CAN'T HELP BUT WONDER
(Where I'm Bound)

Words and Music by
Tom Paxton

Moderately, in 2

It's a long and dust-y road, it's a hot and a heav-y load and the
2. - 5. *See additional lyrics*

folks I meet ain't al-ways kind. Some are bad and some are

good. Some have done the best they could. Some have tried to ease my trou-bl-in'

Copyright © 1963; Renewed 1991 Cherry Lane Music Publishing Company, Inc. (ASCAP) and DreamWorks Songs (ASCAP)
Worldwide Rights for DreamWorks Songs Administered by Cherry Lane Music Publishing Company, Inc.
International Copyright Secured   All Rights Reserved

Chorus

C | Dm | G7 | C Em

mind.   And I can't help but won-der where I'm bound, where I'm

Am | Dm | G7 | C | *To Coda* ⊕ |1.3.

bound,   can't help but won-der where I'm bound.

2. I been
4. And I

2.4. | Dm | G | C Em Am

3. Oh, I
5. If you

2nd time D.S. al Coda

Dm | G | C

52

Additional Lyrics

2. I have wandered through this land just a-doin' the best I can,
   Tryin' to find what I was meant to do.
   And the people that I see look as worried as can be
   And it looks like they are wonderin' too. *(To Chorus)*

3. Oh, I had a little girl one time, she had lips like sherry wine
   And she loved me till my head went plumb insane.
   But I was too blind to see she was driftin' away from me
   And my good gal went off on the morning train. *(To Chorus)*

4. And I had a buddy back home but he started out to roam
   And I hear he's out by 'Frisco Bay.
   And sometimes when I've had a few, his old voice comes singin' through
   And I'm goin' out to see him some old day. *(To Chorus)*

5. If you see me passing by and you sit and you wonder why,
   And you wish that you were a rambler too;
   Nail your shoes to the kitchen door, lace 'em up and bar the door,
   Thank your stars for the roof that's over you. *(To Chorus)*

MOTHER NATURE'S SON

Words and Music by
John Lennon and Paul McCartney

Copyright © 1968 Sony/ATV Songs LLC
Copyright Renewed
All Rights Administered by Sony/ATV Music Publishing, 8 Music Square West, Nashville, TN 37203
International Copyright Secured   All Rights Reserved

Gtr. 1: w/ Rhy. Fill 1, 2nd & 3rd times
E9/G♯ E9 A D/A A D/A A D/A A D/A
son. All day long I'm sit-ting sing - ing songs for ev - 'ry-one.
rise. Lis - ten to the pret-ty sound of mu - sic as she flies.
son. Sway - ing dai - sies sing a la - zy song be-neath the sun.
1.
D F/D G/D D F/D
G/D D
2.
D F/D G/D D Dsus4
Do, doot,
Rhy. Fill 1
Gtr. 1
T
A
B

Bridge
D
Dsus4
G/D
Dmaj7
D7
D13
do, do, do, do,
do, do-dle,
doo - dle, do.
Do, do, do, do,
do, doo - dle,
do.
mm, do, do,
mm, do, do, do, do, do,
To Coda
G(add9)/D
Gm(add9)/D
yeah, yeah, yeah.
D.S. al Coda
(take 2nd ending)
Coda
Verse
4. Mm,
mm,
Gtr. 1
Gtr. 2 (acous.)
let ring
mf

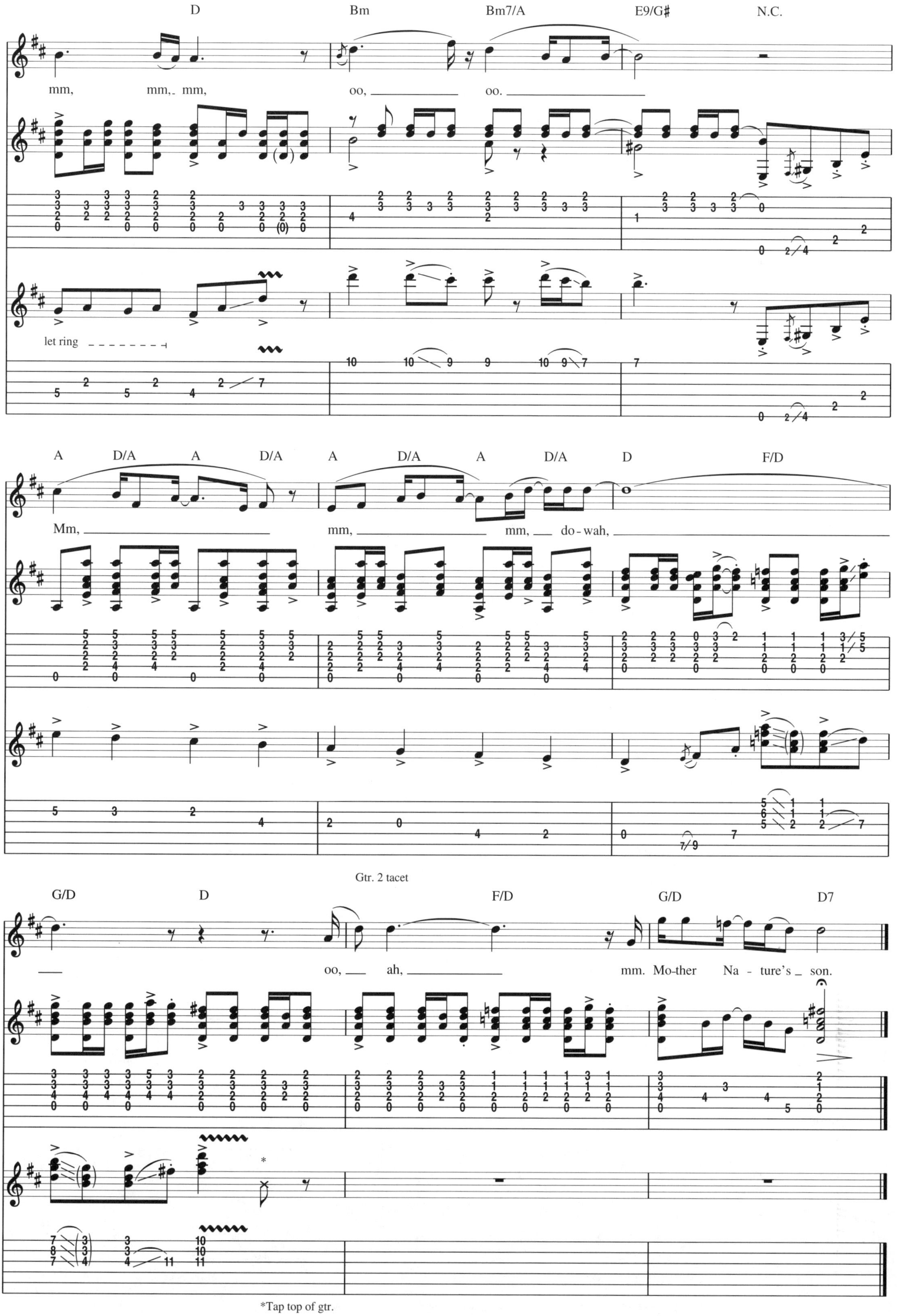

*Tap top of gtr.

WILLIN'

Words and Music by
Lowell George

Open G tuning:
(low to high) D–G–D–G–B–D

Intro
Moderately slow ♩ = 72

℠ **Verse**

1. I been warped __ by the rain, driv-en by the snow. I'm
   kicked by the wind, __ robbed by the sleet, had my

drunk and dirt-y, don't ya know, __ and I'm still will-in'. __ And I was
head stoved in but I'm still on my feet, and I'm still will-in'. __ I

out on the road late at night, I seen my pret-ty Al-ice in ev-'ry head-light.
smug-gled some smokes and folks from Mex-i-co, __ baked by the sun ev-'ry time I go to Mex-

Al-ice, Dal-las Al-ice. } And I've been from ___
i-co, and I'm still. }

Chorus

Tus-con to Tu-cum-car-i, Te-hach-a-pi to To-na-pah. __ Driv-en

Copyright © 1970 (Renewed) Naked Snake Music (ASCAP) and Abraham Music (ASCAP)
All Rights Administered by Naked Snake Music
All Rights Reserved

ev-'ry kind of rig that's ev-er been made._____ Driv-en the back roads so I would-n't get

weighed._____ *rit.* And if you give me weed, whites and ___

wine and you show me a _____ sign, _____ I'll be

will-in' ___ to be mov-in'. ___

Piano Solo
Gtr. 1: w/ Rhy. Fig. 1 (2 times)

2. Well, I've been

Coda

mov - in'. ___

NEW YORK, NEW YORK

Words and Music by
Ryan Adams

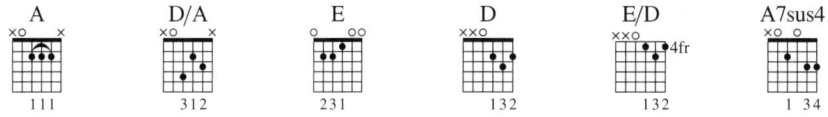

© 2001 BARLAND MUSIC (BMI)/Administered by BUG MUSIC
All Rights Reserved Used by Permission

Verse

Gtr. 1: w/ Rhy. Fig. 1 (4 times)

A   D/A   A

- fled through the cit - y on a Fourth of Ju - ly; ___ I had a fi - re - crack - er wait - in' to blow. ___ Break -
___ my - self a pic - ture that would fit in the folds __ of my wal - let, and it stayed pret - ty good. ___ Still a - mazed __
___ re - mem - ber Christ - mas in the blis - ter - ing cold __ in a church __ on the up - per west side. ___ Babe, __

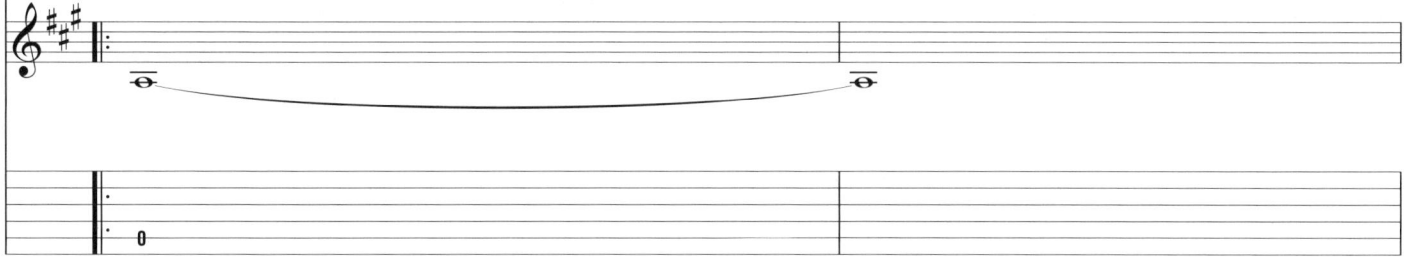

Gtr. 2 tacet

D/A   A

- in' like a rock - et who was mak - in' its way __ to the cit - ies of Mex - i - co. _____ Lived __
___ I did - n't lose it on the roof of the place __ when I was drunk and I was think - in' of you. __ Ev -
___ I stood there sing - in'; I was hold - in' your arm. __ You were hold - in' my trust __ like a child. __ Found __

D/A   A

____ in an a - part - ment out on Av - e - nue A; ___ I had a tar - hut on the cor - ner of Tenth. __ Had ___
- 'ry day the chil - dren, they were sing - in' their tunes __ out on the streets and you could hear from in - side. __ Used __
___ a lot of trou - ble out on Av - e - nue B, ___ but I tried __ to keep the o - ver - head low. __ Fare -

D/A   A

____ my - self a lov - er who was fin - er than gold, ___ but I've - a bro - ken up and bust - ed up since. __
___ to take the sub - way up to Hous - ton and Third; I would wait ____ for you and I'd try to hide. __
- well to the cit - y and the love of my life; ___ least we left ____ be - fore we ___ had to go. ___

Chorus

E   A   E   A

Gtr. 1

Love don't ___ play ___ an - y games with __ me _____ an - y -
Love won't ___ play ___ an - y games with __ you _____ an - y -
Love won't ___ play ___ an - y games with __ you _____ an - y -

61

2nd & 3rd times, Gtr. 2: w/ Fill 1
D
E/D
more, like she did be - fore.
more, if you don't want 'em to.
more, if you don't want 'em to.
So
Gtr. 2
E
A
World won't wait, so I bet - ter shake that thing
World won't wait and I watched you shake, but
we bet - ter shake this old thing out the door. I'll
2nd & 3rd times, Gtr. 2: w/ Fill 2
To Coda
right out there through the door.
hon - ey, I don't blame you.
al - ways be think - in' of you.
Hell, I still love you, New York.
Hell, I still love you, New York.
I'll al - ways love you, though, New York.
(cont. in slashes)
Fill 1
Gtr. 2
*Play cue notes 3rd time.
Fill 2
Gtr. 2

Hell, I __ still love __ you, New York. __

New York. __

I'll al - ways love __ you though, __ New York. __

I'll al - ways love __ you though, __ New York. __

I'll al - ways love __ you though, __ New York. __   New York, __ New York.

Outro

NO SUCH THING

Words by John Mayer
Music by John Mayer and Clay Cook

Intro
Moderately fast Rock ♩ = 132

Emaj9   E

Rhy. Fig. 1
Gtr. 1 (acous.)

Gtr. 1: w/ Rhy. Fig. 1

Emaj9   E   Emaj9

End Rhy. Fig. 1 Gtr. 2 (elec.)

w/ clean tone

Verse
Gtr. 2 tacet
2nd time, Gtr. 3: w/ Riff A (16 times)
1st time, Gtr. 3: w/ Riff A (15 times)

Amaj9

1. "Wel - come to the real ___ world," she said to me con - de - scend -
2. So the good ___ boys and girls ___ take the so - called right track,

Gtr. 1

Riff A
*Gtr. 3 (elec.)

w/ clean tone

Kybd. arr. for gtr.

Copyright © 2001 Specific Harm Music (ASCAP) and Me Hold You Music (ASCAP)
International Copyright Secured All Rights Reserved

C♯m7
ing - ly. "Take a seat, take your life.
fad - ed white hats, grab - bing cred - its and may - be trans - fers. They
P.M.
*T = Thumb on 6th string
Em7add11 Em7 Em9
2nd time, Gtr. 2: w/ Fill 1
Emaj7
Plot it out in black and white." Well, I
read all the books but they can't find the an - swers. And all of our par -
let ring
P.M.
Fill 1
Gtr. 2
let ring

Amaj9

never lived the dreams of the prom ___ kings ___ and the dra - ma queens. _ I'd like to think the
-ents, they're get - ting old - er. _ I won - der if they've wished for an - y - thing

P.M.---┤ P.M.---┤ P.M. P.M.----┤ P.M.----┤ P.M. P.M.----┤ P.M.----┤ P.M.

C#m7   F#7b5   F#7   F#9

best of me ___ is still hid - ing ___ up my ___ sleeve. _
bet - ter while in their mem -'ries ti - ny trag - e - dies. ___

P.M.----┤ P.M.----┤ P.M. P.M.----┤ P.M.----┤

*
*As before

Pre-Chorus
Asus2   A6/8   Asus2   Amaj9

They love to tell you,

Gtr. 3

Gtr. 1

Rhy. Fig. 2

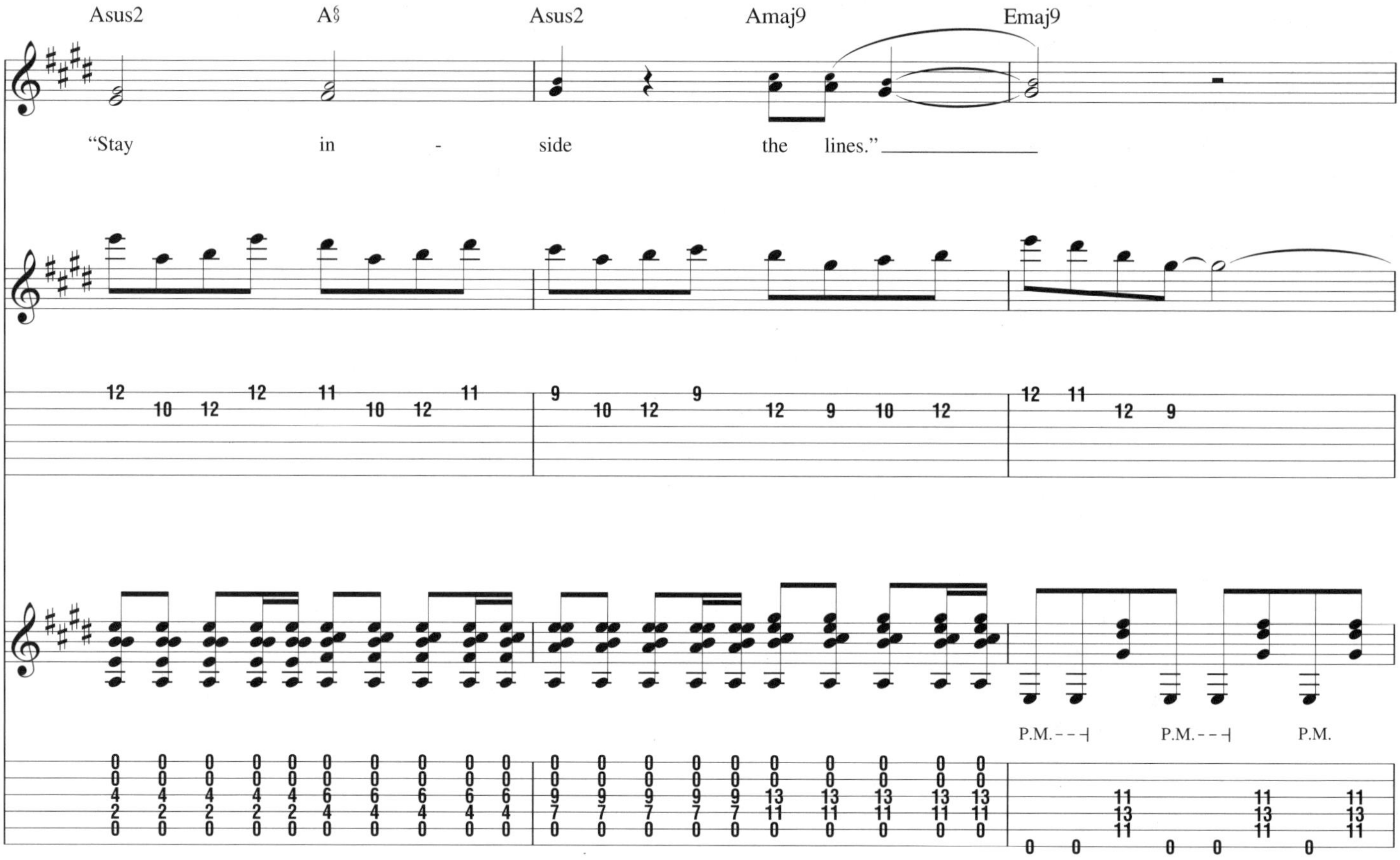

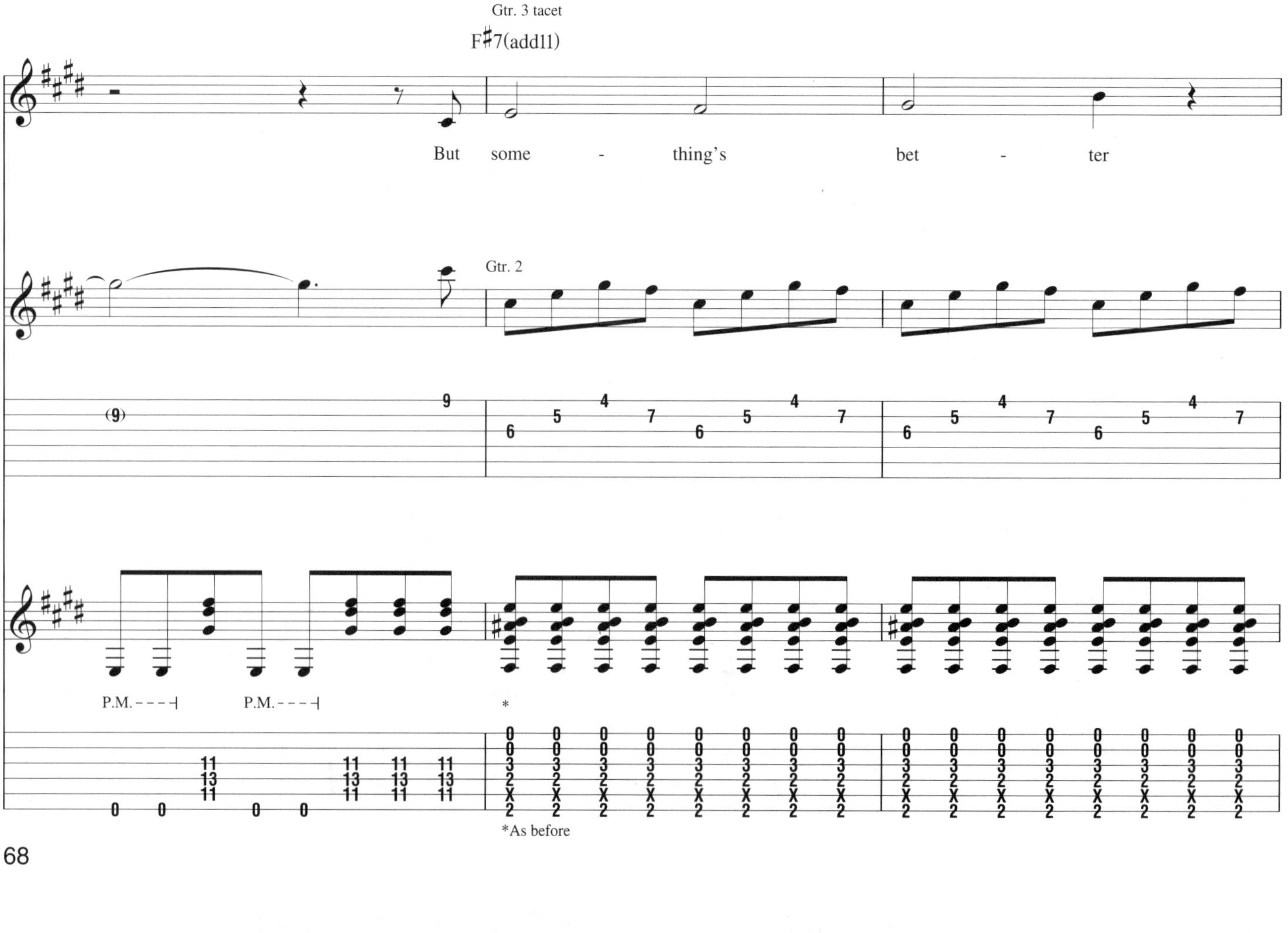

on the oth-er side.

Chorus

Gtr. 2: w/ Riff B (7 times)

I wan-na run through the halls of my high school, I wan-na scream

Riff B

Gtr. 1: w/ Rhy. Fig. 3 (2 times)

Am7add11   D7sus4   Emaj9   Am7add11   D7sus4   Emaj9

____ at the top of my lungs. ____ I just found out ____ there's no such thing as the real ____

1.

Gtr. 1: w/ Rhy. Fill 1

Am7add11   D7sus4   Emaj9

____ world,   just a lie ____ you've got to rise ____ a - bove.

2.

Gtr. 1: w/ Rhy. Fig. 3

Am7add11   D7sus4   Emaj9

____ ____ you've got to rise a - bove. ____

Bridge
Half-time feel

Fmaj7#11   Aadd9   Fmaj7#11

*Gtrs. 1 & 2

** *let ring* - - - - - - - - -

*Two gtrs. arr. for one.
    **As before

Rhy. Fill 1

Gtr. 1

70

Aadd9
Fmaj7♯11
Fmaj7
I am in - vin - ci - ble.
I am in - vin -
let ring
Aadd9
Fmaj7♯11
Fmaj7
Fmaj7♯11
Aadd9
ci - ble.
I am in - vin - ci - ble as
let ring
Gtr. 2 tacet
Fadd♯4/G
long as I'm a - live.
Gtr. 1
P.M.
*As before

Guitar Solo

Gtr. 1: w/ Rhy. Fig. 2
Asus2
A6/9
Asus2
Amaj9
Asus2
A6/9
Gtr. 3
Asus2
Amaj9
Emaj9
F♯7(add11)
Asus2
E/G♯
I wan - na run

Chorus

Gtr. 1: w/ Rhy. Fig. 3 (7 times)
Gtrs. 2 & 3: w/ Riffs A & B (15 times)

Am7add11   D7sus4   Emaj9   Am7add11   D7sus4   Emaj9

_____ through the halls _____ of my high _____ school,   I wan - na scream _____ at the top of my lungs. _____

Am7add11   D7sus4   Emaj9

_____   I just found out _____ there's no such thing as the real _____ world,   just a lie _____

Am7add11   D7sus4   Emaj9   Am7add11   D7sus4   Emaj9

_____ you've got to rise a - bove. _____   I just can't wait _____ till my ten _____ year re - un -

Am7add11   D7sus4   Emaj9

- ion, _____   I'm gon - na bust _____ down the dou - ble doors.   And when I stand _____

Am7add11   D7sus4   Emaj9   Am7add11   D7sus4

_____ on _____ these ta - bles be - fore you,   you will know _____ what all this time was

Gtr. 1

```
3  3  3  3   12 12 12 12
5  5  5  5   10 10 10 10
5  5  5  5   0  0  0  0
X  X  X  X   10 10 10 10
5  5  5  5   10 10 10 10
```

Outro

Gtr. 3: w/ Riff A (7 times)

Emaj7

for.

Gtr. 2

let ring

Gtr. 1

Gtr. 3: w/ Fill 2

let ring

let ring

let ring

Fill 2

Gtr. 3

ROCKY MOUNTAIN HIGH

Words and Music by
John Denver and Mike Taylor

Tune down:
⑥ = D

Moderately slow, in 2

(Strum chords shown in TAB)

1. He was born

in the sum-mer of his twen-ty-sev-enth year, com-in'

2.-5. See additional lyrics

sim.

*To play along with recording, place capo at 2nd fret.

Copyright © 1972; Renewed 2000 Cherry Lane Music Publishing Company, Inc. (ASCAP), DreamWorks Songs (ASCAP), Anna
Kate Deutschendorf, Zachary Deutschendorf and Jesse Belle Denver for the U.S.A.
All Rights for DreamWorks Songs, Anna Kate Deutschendorf and Zachary Deutschendorf Administered by
Cherry Lane Music Publishing Company, Inc. (ASCAP)
All Rights for Jesse Belle Denver Administered by WB Music Corp. (ASCAP)
All Rights for the world excluding the U.S.A. Controlled by Cherry Lane Music Publishing Company, Inc. (ASCAP)
and DreamWorks Songs (ASCAP)
International Copyright Secured   All Rights Reserved

home to a place he'd nev-er been_ be-fore._ He left

yes-ter-day_ be-hind_ him,_ you might say he was born_ a-gain._ You might

say he found the key_ for ev-'ry door._ 2. When he

But the Col-o-ra-do Rock-y Moun-tain high,_

I've seen it rain-in' fire—— in—— the sky.—— The

shad-ow from the star-light—— is soft-er than a lull-a-by.——

3rd time to Coda II;
4th time to Coda III

Rock-y Moun-tain high.——————— (In Col-o-ra-do.)——

D.S.(with repeat)
al Coda I

2nd time to Coda I

Rock-y Moun-tain high.——————— (In Col-o-ra-do.)—— 3. He climbed——

Additional Lyrics

2. When he first came to the mountains his life was far away,
   On the road and hangin' by a song.
   But the string's already broken and he doesn't really care.
   It keeps changin' fast, and it don't last for long. *(To 1st Chorus)*

3. He climbed cathedral mountains, he saw silver clouds below.
   He saw everything as far as you can see.
   And they say that he got crazy once and he tried to touch the sun,
   And he lost a friend but kept his memory.

4. Now he walks in quiet solitude the forests and the streams,
   Seeking grace in every step he takes.
   His sight has turned inside himself to try and understand
   The serenity of a clear blue mountain lake.

   2nd Chorus:
   And the Colorado Rocky Mountain high,
   I've seen it rainin' fire in the sky.
   You can talk to God and listen to the casual reply.
   Rocky Mountain high. (In Colorado.)
   Rocky Mountain high. (In Colorado.)

5. Now his life is full of wonder but his heart still knows some fear
   Of a simple thing he cannot comprehend.
   Why they try to tear the mountains down to bring in a couple more,
   More people, more scars upon the land.

   3rd Chorus:
   And the Colorado Rocky Mountain high,
   I've seen it rainin' fire in the sky.
   I know he'd be a poorer man if he never saw an eagle fly.
   Rocky Mountain high.

   4th Chorus:
   It's a Colorado Rocky Mountain high.
   I've seen it rainin' fire in the sky.
   Friends around the campfire and everybody's high.
   Rock Mountain high. (In Colorado.)

TRIPPING BILLIES

Words and Music by
David J. Matthews

Moderately ♩ = 124

Intro

(Percussion)

Gtr. I (acous.)

D/F#   G

w/Rhy. Fig. 1A
Rhy. Fig. 1

D/F#   G

fade in

f

*L.H. fingering

Bm   Aadd4   D/F#   G

sl.

sl.

1.
D/F#   G   Aadd4   Bm   D/F#   G

2.
D/F#   G   Aadd4   Bm   (end Rhy. Fig. 1)

sl.   sl.

sl.   sl.

sl.   sl.

sl.   sl.

Rhy. Fig. 1A (*Gtr. II)   Play 3 times

let ring

let ring

*Clean elec.

Copyright © 1993, 1996 Colden Grey, Ltd. (ASCAP)
International Copyright Secured All Rights Reserved

1st, 2nd, 3rd Verses
w/Rhy. Fig. 2A
A D5 C B5
1. We were a - bove, you were stand - ing un - der - neath us. We
2.3. See additional lyrics
Rhy. Fig. 2
let ring
sl.
A D5 D/F♯ G A D5 C
were not yet lov - ers. Drag - ons were smoked, bum -
B5 A D5 D/F♯ G
ble - bees were sting - ing us. I was soon to be cra - zy.
1. Eat, drink
2.3. So why
(end Rhy. Fig. 2)
Rhy. Fig. 2A (Gtr. II)
*Play w/slight variations ad lib on repeat.

Chorus
w/Rhy. Fig. 3A

Bm Aadd4   D/F♯ G Aadd4 Bm Aadd4   Bm Aadd4

___ and   be___ mer - ry,___   for___ to - mor - row we___ die.___
            would you care___   to___ get out of___ this___ place?___

Rhy. Fig. 3

D/F♯ G Aadd4 Bm   Aadd4   D/F♯ G Aadd4 Bm   Aadd4   To Coda ⊕

___   Eat,   drink___ and   be___ mer - ry,___   for___ to -
           You and me___ and   all___ our friends,___   such___ a

(end Rhy. Fig. 3)

*Sing harmony
3rd time only.

Rhy. Fig. 3A (Gtr. II)   Play 3 times

1.
Bm Aadd4 D/F♯ G Aadd4 Bm
mor - row we die. 'Cause we're trip - ping
Rhy. Fill 2
sl. sl.
w/Rhy. Figs. 2 & 2A
A D5 C B5 A D5 D/F♯ G
Bil - lies.
A D5 C B5 A D5 D/F♯ G
2.
w/Rhy. Fill 1
Bm Aadd4 D/F♯ G Aadd4 Bm D/F♯ G
w/Rhy. Figs. 1 & 1A
D/F♯ G
hap - py hu - man race, yeah.
Bm Aadd4 D/F♯ G D/F♯ G Aadd4 Bm D/F♯ G D/F♯ G
Gtr. I substitute Rhy. Fill 2
Bm Aadd4 D/F♯ G D/F♯ G Aadd4 Bm
'Cause we're trip - ping
Rhy. Fill 1 (Gtr. I)
sl. sl.

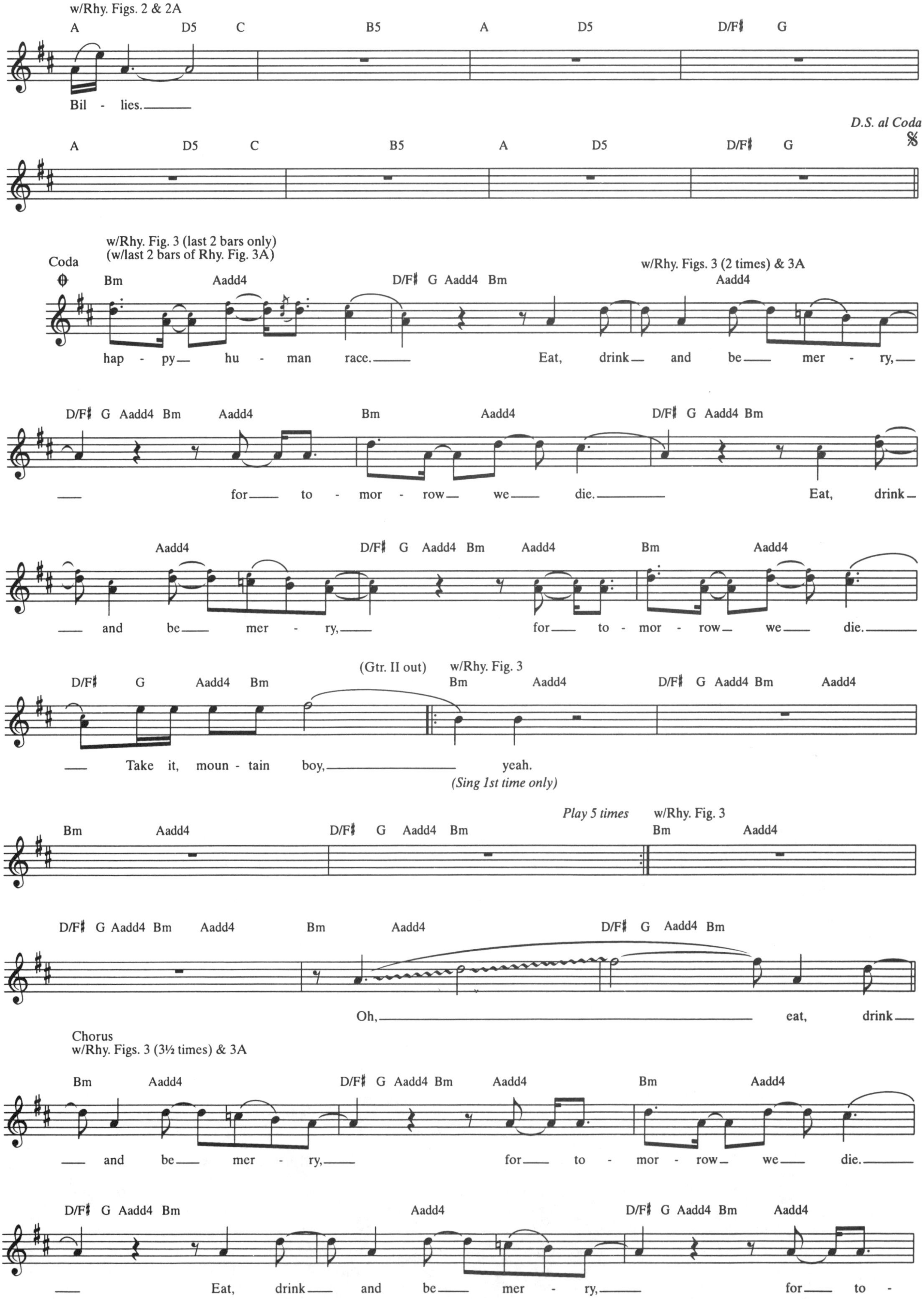
w/Rhy. Figs. 2 & 2A
A D5 C B5 A D5 D/F♯ G
Bil - lies.
A D5 C B5 A D5 D/F♯ G
D.S. al Coda
Coda
w/Rhy. Fig. 3 (last 2 bars only)
(w/last 2 bars of Rhy. Fig. 3A)
Bm Aadd4 D/F♯ G Aadd4 Bm
hap - py human race.
w/Rhy. Figs. 3 (2 times) & 3A
Aadd4
Eat, drink and be mer - ry,
D/F♯ G Aadd4 Bm Aadd4 Bm Aadd4 D/F♯ G Aadd4 Bm
for to - mor - row we die. Eat, drink
Aadd4 D/F♯ G Aadd4 Bm Aadd4 Bm Aadd4
and be mer - ry, for to - mor - row we die.
D/F♯ G Aadd4 Bm
Take it, moun - tain boy,
(Gtr. II out)
w/Rhy. Fig. 3
Bm Aadd4 D/F♯ G Aadd4 Bm Aadd4
yeah.
(Sing 1st time only)
Bm Aadd4 D/F♯ G Aadd4 Bm
Play 5 times
w/Rhy. Fig. 3
Bm Aadd4
D/F♯ G Aadd4 Bm Aadd4 Bm Aadd4 D/F♯ G Aadd4 Bm
Oh, eat, drink
Chorus
w/Rhy. Figs. 3 (3½ times) & 3A
Bm Aadd4 D/F♯ G Aadd4 Bm Aadd4 Bm Aadd4
and be mer - ry, for to - mor - row we die.
D/F♯ G Aadd4 Bm Aadd4 D/F♯ G Aadd4 Bm Aadd4
Eat, drink and be mer - ry, for to -

*Whole rest w/fermata in last bar   *w/echo

Additional Lyrics

2. We're wearing nothing,
   Nothing but our shadows.
   Shadows falling down on the beach sand.
   Remembering once,
   Out on the beaches,
   We wore pineapple grass bracelets. *(To Chorus)*

3. We are all sitting,
   Legs crossed 'round a fire.
   My yellow flame, she dances.
   Tequila drinking,
   Oh, our minds will wander
   To wondrous places. *(To Chorus)*

Guitar Notation Legend

Guitar Music can be notated three different ways: on a *musical staff*, in *tablature*, and in *rhythm slashes*.

RHYTHM SLASHES are written above the staff. Strum chords in the rhythm indicated. Use the chord diagrams found at the top of the first page of the transcription for the appropriate chord voicings. Round noteheads indicate single notes.

THE MUSICAL STAFF shows pitches and rhythms and is divided by bar lines into measures. Pitches are named after the first seven letters of the alphabet.

TABLATURE graphically represents the guitar fingerboard. Each horizontal line represents a string, and each number represents a fret.

4th string, 2nd fret

1st & 2nd strings open, played together

open D chord

HALF-STEP BEND: Strike the note and bend up 1/2 step.

WHOLE-STEP BEND: Strike the note and bend up one step.

GRACE NOTE BEND: Strike the note and immediately bend up as indicated.

SLIGHT (MICROTONE) BEND: Strike the note and bend up 1/4 step.

BEND AND RELEASE: Strike the note and bend up as indicated, then release back to the original note. Only the first note is struck.

PRE-BEND: Bend the note as indicated, then strike it.

VIBRATO: The string is vibrated by rapidly bending and releasing the note with the fretting hand.

WIDE VIBRATO: The pitch is varied to a greater degree by vibrating with the fretting hand.

HAMMER-ON: Strike the first (lower) note with one finger, then sound the higher note (on the same string) with another finger by fretting it without picking.

PULL-OFF: Place both fingers on the notes to be sounded. Strike the first note and without picking, pull the finger off to sound the second (lower) note.

LEGATO SLIDE: Strike the first note and then slide the same fret-hand finger up or down to the second note. The second note is not struck.

SHIFT SLIDE: Same as legato slide, except the second note is struck.

TRILL: Very rapidly alternate between the notes indicated by continuously hammering on and pulling off.

TAPPING: Hammer ("tap") the fret indicated with the pick-hand index or middle finger and pull off to the note fretted by the fret hand.

NATURAL HARMONIC: Strike the note while the fret-hand lightly touches the string directly over the fret indicated.

PINCH HARMONIC: The note is fretted normally and a harmonic is produced by adding the edge of the thumb or the tip of the index finger of the pick hand to the normal pick attack.

PICK SCRAPE: The edge of the pick is rubbed down (or up) the string, producing a scratchy sound.

MUFFLED STRINGS: A percussive sound is produced by laying the fret hand across the string(s) without depressing, and striking them with the pick hand.

PALM MUTING: The note is partially muted by the pick hand lightly touching the string(s) just before the bridge.

RAKE: Drag the pick across the strings indicated with a single motion.

TREMOLO PICKING: The note is picked as rapidly and continuously as possible.

VIBRATO BAR DIVE AND RETURN: The pitch of the note or chord is dropped a specified number of steps (in rhythm) then returned to the original pitch.

VIBRATO BAR SCOOP: Depress the bar just before striking the note, then quickly release the bar.

VIBRATO BAR DIP: Strike the note and then immediately drop a specified number of steps, then release back to the original pitch.

More Terrific Titles from Cherry Lane

THE DAVE MATTHEWS BAND

For a complete listing of Cherry Lane titles available, including contents listings, please visit our web site at www.cherrylane.com

DAVE MATTHEWS BAND–EVERYDAY [INCLUDES TAB]

Matching folio to this recent release by Dave Matthews Band. Includes: Angel • Dreams of Our Fathers • Everyday • Fool to Think • I Did It • If I Had It All • Mother Father • Sleep to Dream Her • So Right • The Space Between • What You Are • When the World Ends.

____02500390 Piano/Vocal/
　　　　　　　Guitar $14.95
____02500389 Play-It-Like-It-Is
　　　　　　　Guitar $19.95

DAVE MATTHEWS BAND – BEFORE THESE CROWDED STREETS [INCLUDES TAB]

Matching songbook to the rockin' five-some's album features all 11 songs, including the hit single "Don't Drink the Water," plus photos and background on the album and the band.

____02501357 Play-It-Like-It-Is
　　　　　　　Guitar $19.95
____02500003 Piano/Vocal/Guitar
　　　　　　　...........................$17.95

DAVE MATTHEWS BAND – CRASH [INCLUDES TAB]

The matching folio to this chart-topping album features all 12 songs, including: Too Much • Crash Into Me • Drive in Drive Out • Proudest Monkey • and more, plus photos and biography.

____02502199 Piano/Vocal/Guitar
　　　　　　　...........................$17.95
____02501279 Play-It-Like-It-Is
　　　　　　　Guitar $19.95

BEST OF THE DAVE MATTHEWS BAND FOR DRUMS

10 songs transcribed for drums, including: Ants Marching • The Best of What's Around • Crash into Me • Satellite • What Would You Say • and more.

____02500184 Play-It-Like-It-Is
　　　　　　　Drum $19.95

DAVE MATTHEWS BAND – JUST THE RIFFS

Over 25 riffs from songs by the Dave Matthews Band. Features: Ants Marching • Crash into Me • Don't Drink the Water • Proudest Monkey • Stay (Wasting Time) • What Would You Say • and more.

____02500019 Just the Riffs
　　　　　　　Guitar w/ Tab $10.95
____02500373 Just the Riffs
　　　　　　　Saxophone..........$9.95
____02500379 Just the Riffs
　　　　　　　Violin $9.95

DAVE MATTHEWS BAND – UNDER THE TABLE AND DREAMING [INCLUDES TAB]

The matching folio to the smash album. Features all 12 songs from the album, including: What Would You Say • The Best of What's Around • Ants Marching • Warehouse • plus photos, a bio, and Dave's comments on the songs.

____02502192 Piano/Vocal/Guitar
　　　　　　　...........................$17.95
____02501266 Play-It-Like-It-Is
　　　　　　　Guitar $19.95

BEST OF DAVE MATTHEWS BAND FOR EASY GUITAR [INCLUDES TAB]

10 of their best arranged for easy guitar, including: Ants Marching • The Best of What's Around • Crash into Me • Crush • Satellite • What Would You Say • and more.

____02500315 Easy Guitar $14.95

DAVE MATTHEWS BAND – LEGENDARY LICKS

This book/CD pack teaches guitarists licks from 11 Dave Matthews Band classics. Includes: Ants Marching • The Best of What's Around • Crash into Me • Crush • Don't Drink the Water • I Did It • Satellite • So Much to Say • Stay (Wasting Time) • Too Much • What Would You Say.

____02500374 Guitar $19.95

DAVE MATTHEWS/ TIM REYNOLDS – LIVE AT LUTHER COLLEGE [INCLUDES TAB]

12 songs from this exciting live performance, including: Ants Marching • Christmas Song • Crash into Me • Deed Is Done • Granny • Minarets • One Sweet World • Satellite • Seek Up • What Would You Say. Includes a great interview with Dave and Tim, photos and a discography.

____02500131 Play-It-Like-It-Is
　　　　　　　Guitar $19.95

BEST OF DAVE MATTHEWS BAND FOR BASS [INCLUDES TAB]

10 great bass songs, including: Ants Marching • The Best of What's Around • Crash into Me • Don't Drink the Water • Rapunzel • Satellite • So Much to Say • Stay (Wasting Time) • Too Much • What Would You Say.

____02500013 Play-It-Like-It-Is
　　　　　　　Bass $17.95

Prices, contents, and availability subject to change without notice.

See your local music dealer or contact:

CHERRY LANE MUSIC COMPANY
6 East 32nd Street, New York, NY 10016

Exclusively Distributed By

HAL•LEONARD®
7777 W. Bluemound Rd. P.O. Box 13819 Milwaukee, WI 53213

0402

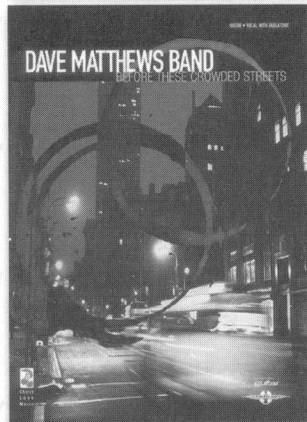

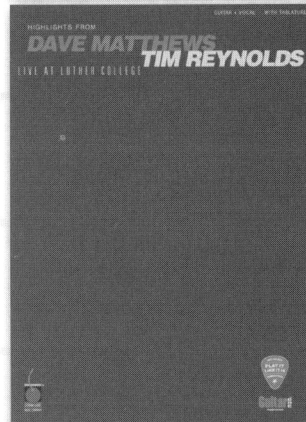

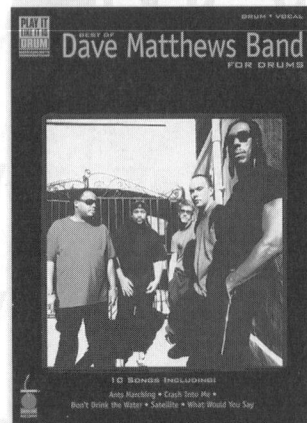

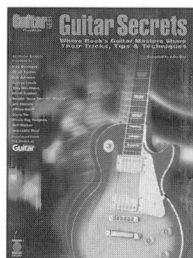

CHERRY LANE MUSIC COMPANY

6 East 32nd Street, New York, NY 10016

Quality in Printed Music

Guitar one™

The Magazine You Can Play

Visit the Guitar One web site at **www.guitarone.com**

ACOUSTIC INSTRUMENTALISTS
INCLUDES TAB

Over 15 transcriptions from legendary artists such as Leo Kottke, John Fahey, Jorma Kaukonen, Chet Atkins, Adrian Legg, Jeff Beck, and more.

02500399 Play-It-Like-It-Is Guitar.............................$9.95

THE BEST BASS LINES
INCLUDES TAB

24 super songs: Bohemian Rhapsody • Celebrity Skin • Crash Into Me • Crazy Train • Glycerine • Money • November Rain • Smoke on the Water • Sweet Child O' Mine • What Would You Say • You're My Flavor • and more.
02500311 Play-It-Like-It-Is Bass $14.95

BLUES TAB
INCLUDES TAB

14 songs: Boom Boom • Cold Shot • Hide Away • I Can't Quit You Baby • I'm Your Hoochie Coochie Man • In 2 Deep • It Hurts Me Too • Talk to Your Daughter • The Thrill Is Gone • and more.
02500410 Play-It-Like-It-Is Guitar...........................$14.95

CLASSIC ROCK TAB
INCLUDES TAB

15 rock hits: Cat Scratch Fever • Crazy Train • Day Tripper • Hey Joe • Hot Blooded • Start Me Up • We Will Rock You • You Really Got Me • and more.
02500408 Play-It-Like-It-Is Guitar...........................$14.95

MODERN ROCK TAB
INCLUDES TAB

15 of modern rock's best: Are You Gonna Go My Way • Denial • Hanging by a Moment • I Did It • My Hero • Nobody's Real • Rock the Party (Off the Hook) • Shock the Monkey • Slide • Spit It Out • and more.
02500409 Play-It-Like-It-Is Guitar...........................$14.95

SIGNATURE SONGS
INCLUDES TAB

21 artists' trademark hits: Crazy Train (Ozzy Osbourne) • My Generation (The Who) • Smooth (Santana) • Sunshine of Your Love (Cream) • Walk This Way (Aerosmith) • Welcome to the Jungle (Guns N' Roses) • What Would You Say (Dave Matthews Band) • and more.
02500303 Play-It-Like-It-Is Guitar...........................$16.95

BASS SECRETS

WHERE TODAY'S BASS STYLISTS GET TO THE BOTTOM LINE
compiled by John Stix

Bass Secrets brings together 48 columns highlighting specific topics – ranging from the technical to the philosophical – from masters such as Stu Hamm, Randy Coven, Tony Franklin and Billy Sheehan. They cover topics including tapping, walking bass lines, soloing, hand positions, harmonics and more. Clearly illustrated with musical examples.
02500100 ....$12.95

CLASSICS ILLUSTRATED

WHERE BACH MEETS ROCK
by Robert Phillips

Classics Illustrated is designed to demonstrate for readers and players the links between rock and classical music. Each of the 30 columns from *Guitar* highlights one musical concept and provides clear examples in both styles of music. This cool book lets you study moving bass lines over stationary chords in the music of Bach and Guns N' Roses, learn the similarities between "Leyenda" and "Diary of a Madman," and much more!
02500101 ....$9.95

GUITAR SECRETS
INCLUDES TAB

WHERE ROCK'S GUITAR MASTERS SHARE THEIR TRICKS, TIPS & TECHNIQUES
compiled by John Stix

This unique and informative compilation features 42 columns culled from *Guitar* magazine. Readers will discover dozens of techniques and playing tips, and gain practical advice and words of wisdom from guitar masters.
02500099 ....$10.95

IN THE LISTENING ROOM

WHERE ARTISTS CRITIQUE THE MUSIC OF THEIR PEERS
compiled by John Stix

A compilation of 75 columns from *Guitar* magazine, *In the Listening Room* provides a unique opportunity for readers to hear major recording artists remark on the music of their peers. These artists were given no information about what they would hear, and their comments often tell as much about themselves as they do about the music they listened to. Includes candid critiques by music legends like Aerosmith, Jeff Beck, Jack Bruce, Dimebag Darrell, Buddy Guy, Kirk Hammett, Eric Johnson, John McLaughlin, Dave Navarro, Carlos Santana, Joe Satriani, Stevie Ray Vaughan, and many others.
02500097 ....$14.95

LEGENDS OF LEAD GUITAR

THE BEST OF INTERVIEWS: 1995-2000

This is a fascinating compilation of interviews with today's greatest guitarists! From deeply rooted blues giants to the most fearless pioneers, legendary players reveal how they achieve their extraordinary craft.
02500329 ....$14.95

LESSON LAB

This exceptional book/CD pack features more than 20 in-depth lessons. Tackle in detail a variety of pertinent music- and guitar-related subjects, such as scales, chords, theory, guitar technique, songwriting, and much more!
02500330 Book/CD Pack....................................$19.95

NOISE & FEEDBACK

THE BEST OF 1995-2000: YOUR QUESTIONS ANSWERED

If you ever wanted to know about a specific guitar lick, trick, technique or effect, this book/CD pack is for you! It features over 70 lessons on composing • computer assistance • education and career advice • equipment • technique • terminology and notation • tunings • and more.
02500328 Book/CD Pack....................................$17.95

OPEN EARS

A JOURNEY THROUGH LIFE WITH GUITAR IN HAND
by Steve Morse

In this collection of 50 *Guitar* magazine columns from the mid-'90s on, guitarist Steve Morse sets the story straight about what being a working musician *really* means. He deals out practical advice on: playing with the band, songwriting, recording and equipment, and more, through anecdotes of his hard-knock lessons learned.
02500333 ....$10.95

SPOTLIGHT ON STYLE

THE BEST OF 1995-2000: AN EXPLORER'S GUIDE TO GUITAR

This book and CD cover 18 of the world's most popular guitar styles, including: blues guitar • classical guitar • country guitar • funk guitar • jazz guitar • Latin guitar • metal • rockabilly and more!
02500320 Book/CD Pack....................................$19.95

STUDIO CITY

PROFESSIONAL SESSION RECORDING FOR GUITARISTS
by Carl Verheyen

In this collection of colomns from Guitar Magazine, guitarists will learn how to: exercise studio etiquette and act professionally • acquire, assemble and set up gear for sessions • use the tricks of the trade to become a studio hero • get repeat call-backs • and more.
02500195 ....$9.95

EXCLUSIVELY DISTRIBUTED BY

HAL•LEONARD® CORPORATION

7777 W. BLUEMOUND RD. P.O. BOX 13819 MILWAUKEE, WI 53213

Visit Cherry Lane online at **www.cherrylane.com**

1101

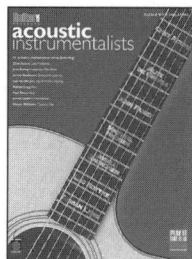

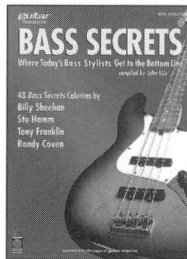

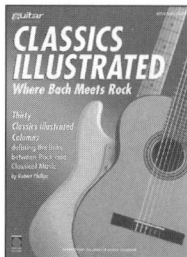

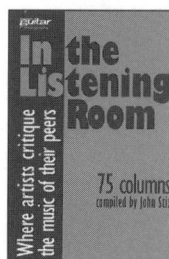

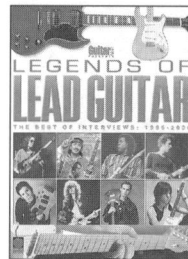

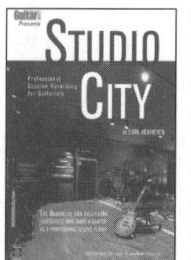

PLAY IT LIKE IT IS GUITAR WITH TABLATURE

NOTE-FOR-NOTE TRANSCRIPTIONS

THE HOTTEST TAB SONGBOOKS AVAILABLE FOR GUITAR & BASS!

PLAY IT LIKE IT IS BASS WITH TABLATURE

NOTE-FOR-NOTE TRANSCRIPTIONS

from

CHERRY LANE MUSIC COMPANY™

Quality in Printed Music

Guitar Transcriptions

02500593	Best of Ryan Adams	$19.95
02500443	Alien Ant Farm – ANThology	$19.95
02501272	Bush – 16 Stone	$21.95
02500193	Bush – The Science of Things	$19.95
02500098	Coal Chamber	$19.95
02500174	Coal Chamber – Chamber Music	$19.95
02500179	Mary Chapin Carpenter – Authentic Guitar Style of	$16.95
02500132	Evolution of Fear Factory	$19.95
02500198	Best of Foreigner	$19.95
02501242	Guns N' Roses – Anthology	$24.95
02506953	Guns N' Roses – Appetite for Destruction	$22.95
02501286	Guns N' Roses Complete, Volume 1	$24.95
02501287	Guns N' Roses Complete, Volume 2	$24.95
02506211	Guns N' Roses – 5 of the Best, Vol. 1	$12.95
02506975	Guns N' Roses – GN'R Lies	$19.95
02500299	Guns N' Roses – Live Era '87-'93 Highlights	$24.95
02501193	Guns N' Roses – Use Your Illusion I	$24.95
02501194	Guns N' Roses – Use Your Illusion II	$24.95
02500458	Best of Warren Haynes	$19.95
02500387	Best of Heart	$19.95
02500007	Hole – Celebrity Skin	$19.95
02501260	Hole – Live Through This	$19.95
02500516	Jimmy Eat World	$19.95
02500554	Jack Johnson – Brushfire Fairytales	$19.95
02500380	Lenny Kravitz – Greatest Hits	$19.95
02500469	Lenny Kravitz – Lenny	$19.95
02500024	Best of Lenny Kravitz	$19.95
02500375	Lifehouse – No Name Face	$19.95
02500558	Lifehouse – Stanley Climbfall	$19.95
02500362	Best of Little Feat	$19.95
02501259	Machine Head – Burn My Eyes	$19.95
02500173	Machine Head – The Burning Red	$19.95
02500305	Best of The Marshall Tucker Band	$19.95
02501357	Dave Matthews Band – Before These Crowded Streets	$19.95
02500553	Dave Matthews Band – Busted Stuff	$22.95
02501279	Dave Matthews Band – Crash	$19.95
02500389	Dave Matthews Band – Everyday	$19.95
02500488	Dave Matthews Band – Live in Chicago 12/19/98 at the United Center, Vol. 1	$19.95
02500489	Dave Matthews Band – Live in Chicago 12/19/98 at the United Center, Vol. 2	$19.95
02501266	Dave Matthews Band – Under the Table and Dreaming	$19.95
02500131	Dave Matthews/Tim Reynolds – Live at Luther College, Vol. 1	$19.95
02500611	Dave Matthews/Tim Reynolds – Live at Luther College, Vol. 2	$19.95
02500529	John Mayer – Room for Squares	$19.95
02506965	Metallica – ...And Justice for All	$22.95
02506210	Metallica – 5 of the Best/Vol.1	$12.95
02506235	Metallica – 5 of the Best/Vol. 2	$12.95
02500070	Metallica – Garage, Inc.	$24.95
02507018	Metallica – Kill 'Em All	$19.95
02501232	Metallica – Live: Binge & Purge	$19.95
02501275	Metallica – Load	$24.95
02507920	Metallica – Master of Puppets	$19.95
02501195	Metallica – Metallica	$22.95
02501297	Metallica – ReLoad	$24.95
02507019	Metallica – Ride the Lightning	$19.95
02500279	Metallica – S&M Highlights	$24.95
02500577	Molly Hatchet – 5 of the Best	$9.95
02501353	Best of Steve Morse	$19.95
02500448	Best of Ted Nugent	$19.95
02500348	Ozzy Osbourne – Blizzard of Ozz	$19.95
02501277	Ozzy Osbourne – Diary of a Madman	$19.95
02509973	Ozzy Osbourne – Songbook	$24.95
02507904	Ozzy Osbourne/Randy Rhoads Tribute	$22.95
02500316	Papa Roach – Infest	$19.95
02500545	Papa Roach – Lovehatetragedy	$19.95
02500194	Powerman 5000 – Tonight the Stars Revolt!	$17.95
02500025	Primus Anthology – A-N (Guitar/Bass)	$19.95
02500091	Primus Anthology – O-Z (Guitar/Bass)	$19.95
02500468	Primus – Sailing the Seas of Cheese	$19.95
02500508	Bonnie Raitt – Silver Lining	$19.95
02501268	Joe Satriani	$22.95
02501299	Joe Satriani – Crystal Planet	$24.95
02500306	Joe Satriani – Engines of Creation	$22.95
02501205	Joe Satriani – The Extremist	$22.95
02507029	Joe Satriani – Flying in a Blue Dream	$22.95
02507074	Joe Satriani – Not of This Earth	$19.95
02500544	Joe Satriani – Strange Beautiful Music	$19.95
02506959	Joe Satriani – Surfing with the Alien	$19.95
02501226	Joe Satriani – Time Machine 1	$19.95
02500560	Joe Satriani Anthology	$24.95
02501255	Best of Joe Satriani	$19.95
02500088	Sepultura – Against	$19.95
02501239	Sepultura – Arise	$19.95
02501240	Sepultura – Beneath the Remains	$19.95
02501238	Sepultura – Chaos A.D.	$19.95
02500188	Best of the Brian Setzer Orchestra	$19.95
02500177	Sevendust	$19.95
02500176	Sevendust – Home	$19.95
02500090	Soulfly	$19.95
02501230	Soundgarden – Superunknown	$19.95
02501250	Best of Soundgarden	$19.95
02500168	Steely Dan's Greatest Songs	$19.95
02500167	Best of Steely Dan for Guitar	$19.95
02501263	Tesla – Time's Making Changes	$19.95
02500583	The White Stripes – White Blood Cells	$19.95
02500431	Best of Johnny Winter	$19.95
02500199	Best of Zakk Wylde	$22.95
02500517	WWE – Forceable Entry	$19.95
02500104	WWF: The Music, Vol.3	$19.95

Bass Transcriptions

02500008	Best of Bush	$16.95
02505920	Bush – 16 Stone	$19.95
02506966	Guns N' Roses – Appetite for Destruction	$19.95
02500504	Best of Guns N' Roses for Bass	$14.95
02500013	Best of The Dave Matthews Band	$17.95
02505911	Metallica – Metallica	$19.95
02506982	Metallica – ...And Justice for All	$19.95
02500075	Metallica – Garage, Inc.	$24.95
02507039	Metallica – Kill 'Em All	$19.95
02505919	Metallica – Load	$19.95
02506961	Metallica – Master of Puppets	$19.95
02505926	Metallica – ReLoad	$21.95
02507040	Metallica – Ride the Lightning	$17.95
02500288	Metallica – S&M Highlights	$19.95
02500347	Papa Roach – Infest	$17.95
02500539	Sittin' In with Rocco Prestia of Tower of Power	$19.95
02500025	Primus Anthology – A-N (Guitar/Bass)	$19.95
02500091	Primus Anthology – O-Z (Guitar/Bass)	$19.95
02500500	Best of Joe Satriani for Bass	$14.95
02500317	Victor Wooten Songbook	$19.95

Transcribed Scores

02500361	Guns N' Roses Greatest Hits	$24.95
02500282	Lenny Kravitz – Greatest Hits	$24.95
02500496	Lenny Kravitz – Lenny	$24.95
02500424	Best of Metallica	$24.95
02500283	Joe Satriani – Greatest Hits	$24.95

FOR MORE INFORMATION, SEE YOUR LOCAL MUSIC DEALER, OR WRITE TO:

HAL•LEONARD® CORPORATION

7777 W. BLUEMOUND RD. P.O. BOX 13819 MILWAUKEE, WI 53213

Prices, contents and availability subject to change without notice.

0303